Parenting for New Dads:

A Survival Guide
for Parenting for New Dads

Table of Contents

Introduction..1

Fatherhood 101..2

What to Expect When You're Completely Lost… 5

The Hour is Upon Us...11

Back to the Home Front..17

The First Three Months..21

Past the First Obstacle 25

Getting Through the First Year...29

Past Year One 33

The Toddler..36

Beyond! 40

Introduction

I want to thank for purchasing the book, Parenting for New Dads.

This book contains proven steps and strategies on how to get the facts about what to expect as a new dad.

Are you tired of having nothing but weird books trying to explain what it's like for a woman to push a small human being out of her body? Do you just want to know what it is you need to start doing? Do you want an honest, completely real perspective from someone who isn't going to bog you down in anatomy that sounds like they're trying to cast spells? Do you just need someone to give it to you straight about what it's like being a dad?

Then you've found the right book. This is the book that's going to give you an honest and realistic look at what's sitting on the horizon. No birthing explanations or fundamentals of the female anatomy here. We're here to give you a heads up on the realities of having a pregnant wife and what to expect as a father. So buckle up for some straight talk and some great information to help you prepare for the greatest transition your life could possibly have. Welcome to fatherhood.

Thanks again for downloading this book, I hope you enjoy it!

Fatherhood 101

Fatherhood is not for the faint of heart. Seriously, every day you're given a ticket to the greatest show on earth, only it's an audience participation show. You're given the wonderful chance to bring in the next generation and mold the mind of a young soul who will grow up to do wondrous and miraculous things. Or maybe not. Really, it all starts right here, right now. You're lucky to be here, but it comes with so much more responsibility than anyone can ever tell you. You really won't comprehend it until you've experienced it, which really won't be long now.

But don't be scared.

You're being smart about it. You wouldn't be reading this book if you weren't anticipating what's coming. You wouldn't have bought this book, you wouldn't have opened the program to read it, and you certainly wouldn't have made it to the second paragraph if you're not a little freaked out and a little nervous about what's coming. That's fine. I was there once too.

God, do I wish that there had been a book out there that catered for men that was just honest. I didn't want statistics and numbers. I didn't want to know exactly what my wife was going through. Heck, I was there at every appointment she would let me in for and I was still learning things that ultimately, I wasn't going to apply in any other way than: Your wife is experiencing discomfort your tiny, masculine brain will not comprehend.

Good.

Check!

Got that the moment she started throwing up in the morning.

What I needed was someone to be real with me, to tell me that everything was going to be alright and that there are some major things that I need to get done before two weeks when that little bundle of joy is getting ready to come out. But that's just the beginning. There's so much afterwards that I wanted to know. I wanted a how to tome explaining everything to me, but I didn't have that. By the time I knew that I needed that information, I was already in the thick of it. It's like deciding when you're dropping into Normandy that you probably should have read the operation manual. So that's what this book is about. This is a guide for you to know what you should expect preparing for this child coming into your life.

It's going to give you a heads up at the fairly universal part of parenting, all the way up to when they enter the precious years known as the toddler years. I'm going to give you all the hints and the suggestions that I would have wished that I had known back then. Strap in and be prepared to take a few notes, because it's going to be a goldmine for you in the future.

The important thing, however, is to remember that being a father is new to everyone and it's extremely scary to anyone. You're going to come to learn fairly quickly that men who are already fathers love to give expecting dads a hard time. They love to scare you, freak you out, and watch you squirm. But the truth is, those fathers who have already tread the narrow, hallowed ground of fatherhood, have a wealth of experience that they'll love to share with you. So please, take my knowledge, take my advice, and do with it whatever you can. You're going to need it in the years to come.

But more important than that, you're going to need to be ready to savor every last second. If you don't get any farther into this book than the introduction, take this away. Savor every precious moment that's to come because they will never be that small, that innocent, that adorable, and that wonderful ever again. They're going to grow and change and they're going to only get better and better, but these few moments you have with your child right now. Savor every blow out diaper, every early morning sing along session back to sleep, and every time they scream at the top of their lungs in the middle of the checkout line. Savor them, because you are their everything and they depend one hundred percent on you and think that you're god right now.

Don't disappoint them.

It's time to step up and I'm more than willing to show you how it's done.

What to Expect When You're Completely Lost...

So, the baby is on the way. Right now, you've probably seen something that looks like a really large bean with legs and arms squirming around inside your wife or girlfriend's stomach and then they put the microphone up to her stomach and then it got real. You heard the heartbeat. You heard life. You heard what is going to fill your eyes with tears and your heart with awe and wonder.

If you haven't experienced it yet, it's powerful. It's coming.

I'm going to jump in right now with the first thing you're going to need to do and we'll take it from here.

<u>Attend Everything!</u>

Seriously get this through your head right now! You attend every doctor's meeting with your wife or girlfriend or fiancé that you can. There are plenty of reasons for this, but ultimately, she is terrified. She is growing a human life inside of her and her body is shifting and changing in ways that we men will never comprehend or understand. I mean, I would feel like the first guy to die in any alien movie if I were here and that would freak me out. The puking every night or morning, or whenever your body decides that it's puke-time. Not only is she going to need you there for support, but she's going to try her hardest to make you feel like you don't have to be there.

She'll say things like: "I know you're busy at work, don't worry about it." Or "It's just a little check up, I'll be fine." But persist my brothers! Persist and you'll inevitably get to the: "Oh, okay, thanks Babe!" stage. She's truly going to want you there and it shows that you're trying your hardest to put forward the white-knight effort. Go for her, but more importantly, there's another reason.

When that baby is born, you are going to be the closest to God that you've ever been. That sweet little bundle of flesh, blood, poop, and pure joy is going to look to you for everything. You are the provider, protector, sustainer, and savior of absolutely everything. For those narcissists out there, it's a horrifying experience that we've been asking for forever. So when you go to those doctor's appointments, ask every question that you can think of. Ask them any concerns that you have and don't talk yourself out of it. Knowledge is your power and anything that keeps your woman happy and healthy is a bonus for you.

So attend everything. Suck the marrow from these doctors and nurses. You're paying them ridiculous amounts of money to tell you the baby is healthy and that all your worries were for nothing, so utilize them. They're going to be more than happy to help you through any concerns that you have.

Nesting

Pregnant women usually hit a phase that's called nesting. It's cute, because they usually hit it at the end of the pregnancy. Most men I know, we hit that the moment we hear the words: "I'm pregnant." I know that I was immediately tallying up the exorbitant costs that were coming our way and I was having a heart attack. So much money, so much work that needs to be done, and so very little time.

Take a moment and relax.

We're men. Our minds are wired to fix things and that's what you're trying to do when you're thinking about how you're going to need to paint the nursery and find out how to paint cute little animals on the walls. Take a moment and just relax and get organized.

Yes, you should definitely be planning on filling your nursery and establishing everything that you're going to need. Making a list of all the things that you need and that you're actually going to need the moment you bring your baby home are two completely different things. Here is what I tell the fathers-to-be that I know. You should buy things by what you're going to need in direct chronological order of when your child is born and be aware of what other people are going to get you. The big things that you're going to need up front:

The Car Seat: If there is one thing that you should be willing to drop money on, it's your car seat. This thing will protect them and save their lives if anything happens to you while you're driving. Invest in a quality car seat that comes with a stroller as well. Don't try to match a car seat to a different stroller. You're begging for a nightmare with that. They're expensive and if you want to save yourself some hassle later on in life, buy a base for each car you have. Then you won't have to switch out the base whenever you need to take a different car. But, that's optional.

A bassinet: For the first two to three months, depending upon when your child transitions over, this is what they're going to be sleeping in. Forget buying the crib immediately. Sure, they're super expensive, but you're going to have two to three extra months to get that crib from the moment you hold your child for the first time. Invest in a good bassinet first.

A rocker: Sometimes, your child doesn't want to sleep in a bassinet. Getting them to sleep is ridiculously painful sometimes when you're waking up every two to three hours. Have a rocker to give your child some diversity. Doctors will tell you that you should limit rockers to naps and not actually sleeping, well, guess what: newborns only nap. They never sleep for significant amounts of time. So do whatever works to give that baby the chance to sleep normally.

A bouncer: Bouncers are rockers that rock only when there's movement involved. This is often a great alternative and I know that my children have all loved their bouncer. I ended up buying this late with my first and I was kicking myself all the way home. You can have your sweet child sleeping and napping by you no matter what time of day it is.

A Changing Table: Some people roll their changing table and baby's dresser into one. I did this and I don't regret it at all. It holds her clothes and I changed her diapers on top. It's a multi-tool. Get a changing pad on top of the changing table, they're super common. It gives your baby comfort while you're changing them and you want them to be comfortable.

Clothes and Diapers: Get used to buying a lot of them and just get it over with early. If you see a really good deal on diapers and clothes, go ahead and buy them. You'll need them in the future. Particularly onesies. You'll never have enough of them. They'll have diaper blowouts and stain them to uselessness and you're just going to want to throw them away. As for diapers, don't waste time buying them in the plastic packs. Start getting the cardboard boxes of like one hundred. You'll be going through them like candy at a parade.

Blankets: You'll never have enough snugglie, warm blankets for you little bundle of joy.

I would suggest getting your crib last, the paint, and anything else that you think you're going to need last. These are the core things that you're going to want to have in your nursery when that baby comes home.

Savior and Slave

Pregnancy sucks. I'm not going to lie about anything involved with it. Every pregnancy is like a unique little nightmare designed specifically for your wife to endure for the seven or eight months after she notices that something's up. It's a miserable time and she's definitely going to show you that she's not happy. For you, it's not very fun either.

You're going to watch your beautiful, sexy, breathtaking woman transform into a miserable, exhausted, uncomfortable vessel for your unborn child. Essentially, they're a meat car for your baby to drive around. It's a terrible and painful which means that you're going to need to be the best that you can for her. She needs you to be supporting and nurturing to her as she goes through this.

The best advice that I can give you is to read the situation. If you're smothering her or she needs time away form you for a while, give it to her. The desire to fight with her and tell her how unreasonable she is being is so tempting, but don't give in. Be the bigger person. Nothing you say can end well for you. You just need to let her be for a while and just move on. Do what you can to make things easier. Get used to doing as much work as you possibly can and carrying a bigger load. Nothing is ever going to get easier from this point, so jump in wherever you can.

It might feel like you're being a slave, but you're being her savior. You're helping keep her sanity and that's what's important at this point. Just help her, bear the lack of gratitude, and know that eventually, it will get much better. She's going to remember all the work that you've done for her over these months and a happy mother helps make a happy baby, or so some old people have said.

When it comes to being a father expecting, the only thing you really can do is prepare. You can prepare a lot and you can stress for it, but don't forget to be present and with her through all of this time. She needs you and don't ever lose sight of that. Help her however you can and make these days easier for her so that you're both ready and prepared for when the baby arrives. Just cherish these moments with just the two of you and be prepared for your life to change on so many levels. Again, take it easy. You have time. Research and learn as much as you can with your spare time.

The Hour is Upon Us

Before we go any further into this rabbit hole, let me get one thing out in the open and cleared up before you faint or have a heart attack thinking about that horrifying trip to the hospital. Oh God, will you make it in time? How will you deliver the baby? What if you get hit by a car trying to catch the light? What happens if a sink hole opens up and swallows the road? You've seen it in movies and you've heard stories about it. So clearly it's a possibility, right?

No.

Well, maybe, but let's stick with no.

The point is, what you need to know is that it's nothing like the movies. Especially since this is your first child, the moment contractions start to happen and it looks like labor is coming, you're going to be checking that app you downloaded every few minutes, timing it like a pro. When your wife says it's time to go, then you're going to load up into the car and you're going to head to triage, aka the tenth ring of hell. So don't worry about not making it to the hospital on time. That's just something humorous writers use on television and in movies. Besides, if you're anything like me, you'll probably drive the route from your home to the hospital a few times just to time it.

But before that happens, the first thing you need to know and have ready for this little adventure is a game plan. Pack a hospital bag and have it with your wife at all times. Especially once you get into that eighth month. This is a hospital bag that will be full of everything that your wife is going to need to be comfortable—as much as possible—and things you'll need for the baby. This is stuff like a onesie, some pajamas for both the baby and your wife, a blanket for both, slippers for your wife, make up for when visitors come, and anything that your wife needs. Honestly, sit down one night and make an event out of it. Have fun with it and make sure you go over it again and again, just in case. Once you have it figured out, it stays near your wife at all times. Because when it's go time, she's going to need it.

So, when that little bundle of joy burning up inside your wife who is now swollen and exhausted from all of this, decides to come shooting out, it's very slow. Seriously, we're talking hours. There are a lot of ways to induce labor to try and get it going faster and I'm sure your doctor has told you already. There's walking, mild exercise, sex, and a whole slew of foods that you can eat to try and get this thing going. It's going to take a while, but it will eventually come for you. When it does come, it's time to start timing the contractions.

Honestly, they say to wait until you have stable contractions lasting around a minute and most doctors say not to worry until they're three to four minutes apart before heading to the hospital. As for you, you're probably going to want to head there as soon as possible. Do whatever you feel comfortable doing, just know that hospitals are extremely uncomfortable and don't really cater to you until you're admitted into triage. Get there whenever you feel it's time for you to start moving in that direction.

Once you're at the hospital, it's time to check in. All of my children started coming in the middle of the night, which is pretty peaceful because we had a lot of the wing to ourselves and two other couples. During the day, it's an entirely different scene. It's busier, but essentially, it all comes down to the same. What you have ahead of you is a lot of waiting.

Seriously, so much waiting. Triage is the closest thing that you're ever going to come to that resembles hell. You're going to be sitting around while your wife suffers over and over again trying to manage the pain. There's a lot of pain and suffering that is going all throughout that room and it's permeating everything. With you sitting there, you're going to feel like you're just there for one thing and that one thing is keeping your wife comfortable. Why? Because that's the only reason you have to be here.

That's honestly the only thing that is keeping you there, because you have to have, an amazing and wonderful ability to try and ease that unimaginable pain. Remember, that the word I'm using there is "try." That's because there's something impossible about this objective, you need to understand right now that you're going to fail. There is no way that you can ever succeed in this goal. There's nothing in the world that can alleviate her from the pain that she's going through. So whatever you think you can do to help her is a must at that moment. Get her ice, get her something to drink, or do whatever you can for her. So do whatever you can for her and do it immediately.

There's a moment where you're going to understand the true reason for the existence of triage and that's to drive your wife insane and you're in shotgun with her. So whenever you can, get her up and get her walking, get her moving to help her dilate. So get her up and get her walking as much as you can. You want to help her dilate as much as possible and other than that, you're just there to keep her company and keep her mildly comfortable.

Other than that, the reality of your life at this moment is to just be there. So, from this moment on, until you leave the hospital, you're there as a helper and a guide for the woman you love.

Now, let's talk about the room. There are a lot of people that are taking the different approach to being in the room. A lot of women don't want to have their husband, boyfriend, or man in the same room with them as they're giving birth. There's also the reality that a lot of men don't want to be in the room when their wife is giving birth. This is, of course, a decision that you and your wife should make up before you're in the hospital. You should discuss the reality of whether you want to be present at the birth or if you want to wait outside the room.

Here's the reason why you might want to opt out of being in the room. One, you're not actually doing anything in there. You're standing by, watching as people work—working to ensure that your wife and your child are going to survive this entire experience. You're dead weight and that's just the physical part of. The emotional part is a tremendous consideration as well. You're watching your wife go through the most traumatic event she's had to experience up to this point. It's traumatic for both of you. And if you're not present, you still get the chance to come swooping in and hold your baby within seconds of that little darling being born.

Of course, there are also benefits to witnessing your child being born and the option to cut the umbilical cord if that's something you're interested in. A lot of men feel pressured into doing so, but don't worry, you're not a bad father if you don't. The point of this is that you should not be having this conversation and making this decision with your wife in the middle of triage. Have a plan so that when they move your wife to her room, you're ready to spring into action.

Once you're in the room, it's only a matter of time. There's always a chance that this could be false labor and that you could be turning around in a few hours and heading back home, still pregnant, so do what you can to help her. Get her up and have her take walks when she feels like she can, but when the moment is right, they're going to inject her with the epidural anesthesia.

This is a terrifying moment for you because epidurals are incredible dangerous if done wrong, but they're a blessing to women who get them. The pain alleviates and everything starts to flow a little smoother. By this point, her water will have either been broken for her or will have broken on its own. Most women actually have their water broken by their doctor, so don't be alarmed if it's not happening. Once you're at this point, there's no going back.

When your child is born, it's going to be the most incredible moment in your life. If there's one thing that I can stress to you as a father is to just be present. Soak this in and remember absolutely everything you can. You want this moment to stick with you until the day you die. When you're wife is done crying and holding her precious baby, then it's up to you. This is the first time that you'll be your child's guardian and protector.

For the sanity of your wife and for yourself, do not let the nurses take your baby anywhere without you. Be there for that child. They are so innocent and so alone in the world and everything is so new and scary for them that your face and your voice needs to be there as a comfort for them. Since you're a loving father, you've undoubtedly been talking to your child while they were in the womb and they know your voice very well by now. Be there for them—comfort them. They're so small and so precious that you'll gladly do it.

Congratulations, you're now a father.

Back to the Home Front

After your wife has given birth, you're entirely overwhelmed with so many things that it's almost impossible to bottle them all up into ink and spread them across a page. You're going to have people going in and out of your room all the time, people working there and people who are coming to visit you. You're going to stay up all night with your wife, staring at your precious new little member of your family. Everyone is going to be eager to see you, your wife, and most of all, your sweet little child. It's going to be a daze of confusion and excitement. Everything from the first diaper, the first bath, and the first feeding is all going to happen right there in that room. It's an amazing little room and you're never going to forget it.

But eventually, you have to go home.

Driving home from the hospital is going to be the slowest and the safest that you've ever driven in your life. Paranoia is going to swarm you like a mad horde of locust and every intersection is going to drive you mad. You're carrying your newborn child and at this point, everything is real. The fact that you're a father, that a child is so innocent and so fragile, and that your wife is still exhausted from giving birth. Everything is incredibly terrifying on your way home and the moment that you pull into your garage is going to be the most satisfying moment in your life.

At home, hopefully you have been making the most of the time that you've had leading up to this point and that you're fully stocked and prepared for your new arrival. With your house ready and fully stocked for your little bundle of joy, then you're ready for them. Of course, that's when the fear and the terror really gets to sink in for you. So now that you have the moment to put everything to use.

Now that you're home, it might be scary to think that you have the whole responsibility of taking care of your child all by yourself. Now, no matter how horrifying and absolutely disturbing this might seem to you, it's still the reality of the situation. Your child is entirely in your care now. But it's not as horrifying as you might think it is.

The average newborn sleeps somewhere around twenty hours a day. That's a lot of sleeping time that you're going to spend watching them dream peacefully, completely enchanted by their very existence. It's hard not to feel completely enamored and seduced by this little being that has officially become king or queen of the house you once occupied. Right now, your main concern is going to be feeding.

Newborns hardly eat anything and sleeping is pretty much all they do for the first two weeks. Waking up and light is really the hardest part for them to cope with. Hunger is quite possibly the worst thing that they can experience outside of physical pain. When a child is in the womb, they are constantly satiated by their mother's snacking and eating. It's a steady stream of yummies heading straight to their tummy, but that's not the case anymore.

I remember that my father told me something when I was waiting for my first child to arrive. He enlightened me to the reality of what a newborn experiences. Every great pleasure that a newborn experiences is singlehandedly the greatest thing they've experienced and every horrible feeling is literally the worst. Think about it. Everything is new to them. So right now, you want to keep your beloved heart and soul happy and comfortable. Feeding them is going to be the hardest because they want to sleep so much. Waking up a sleeping newborn to feed is going to be a pain in the butt, because a lot of the times, they just don't want to. Don't worry about it, a newborn will definitely tell you when it's hungry. They're more than great at communicating that to you.

If your wife has decided to breast feed or go the formula route, you're in the throes of feeding adventures. I'm going to tell you upfront that no matter what pop study you're reading or what this celebrity or that said in an interview, there is really no distinguishable difference between formula and breast milk. Statistics are like puppets, they can be made to say whatever you want. So don't feel bad if you're doing formula runs in the middle of the night or someone gives you the death's glare for feeding your child formula. If you have any say in the matter, I would suggest to your wife that every time in the middle of the night your child wants to eat, it's going to require her attention unless you start pumping. In the end, it's painful and a hassle for your wife.

As you can probably tell, we went the formula route for medical reasons. It's messy and it's all lady trouble, so I won't go into details, but my children are happy, smiling beauties and they're doing just fine. My niece, she was breast fed and turned out just as great too. So the decision is up to you.

But in the end, diapers are where you're going to be spending most of your time. Diapers are disgusting, monotonous, and are quickly going to become second nature to you. The first diaper is going to be tricky, but by the end of the second day, you'll be as professional as you can imagine. In the end, coming home is about getting into that routine, because it's only going to get better from here on out.

The First Three Months

So baby is home and happy and mommy is on her way to recovering. What lies ahead is the long road of fatherhood and there's no looking back. By the time you get to this point, there is going to be a profound transition of who you are. I think every man goes through it once they have a child, though the time varies from man to man. But the point is that you are now a father and you're going to be noticing everything that this entails.

The first three months of fatherhood are kind of like you've been given the responsibility of a lifetime and all you can do is think about them as they suck away the sleep and time. Don't think of this as a downer. You'll spend hours just staring at your child and you'll wake up at ridiculous hours to make sure that they're hungry, dry, and happy with more enthusiasm than you would have thought. But you'll still be operating in a haze of exhaustion and sleep deprivation. Essentially, you are just making sure that your baby stays alive.

Don't worry, the time is going to shoot by.

So once again, make sure that you're savoring every last moment that you have with your precious baby. Here are some of the things that you're going to encounter along the way and that you're going to be in charge of.

The first is naps. For the most part, the first three months are going to be periods of adjustment for the baby. A baby has no understanding of night and day, so they sleep when they want and they wake up when they want. For the first two months, there's not a lot that you're going to be able to do to change this. Whether you're going have them nap in a bassinet, a rocker, or a bouncer, your baby is going to dictate when and where they'll be laying their head for the night. But right around the third month, you can start to adjust their sleeping patterns to be a little more normal to your schedule.

As far as naps go, swaddling is the key component for getting your child to sleep. Especially as they start to move their hands and feet more. Children begin to gain control of their body from the head down and they start to move from the head down. So it's going to start with the head, followed by the arms, and then the legs will start kicking. Now, since a newborn is just getting acquainted to all of these limbs, they're going to be keeping themselves awake with these movements. Swaddling is the one skill you're going to have to fight that. Swaddling is something you'll have down in the first week or so. So make sure you have plenty of blankets.

Remember, lay your child on their back when they sleep and when you get to the point that you're acquainting them with their crib, right in the beginning or middle of the second month for naps, make sure you have a mobile for them to get interested in. Babies are fascinated by mobiles or anything that hangs above them. Be sure that you constantly monitor your child and make sure that they're safe during their naps and be certain that blankets have not fallen over their faces.

Another thing that you're going to be learning is how to give your child a bath. At first, make sure that you have a baby bath. For the first three months, children are really starting to awaken their motor skills and are unable to truly move effectively. Bathing them is all up to you and it's going to be for a few years, so get used to it. It's a complete blast. All newborns react differently to baths. Some love them, others hate them. It's your job to make sure that they're completely clean though, so get in there and scrub them. I know that this really goes without saying, but never leave your child unattended near water. Don't walk away, don't run to grab something, and even if the President is at your door, you don't leave your child alone in the bath. Pretty basic stuff.

Now, something that's huge during the first three months is you bonding with your child. Every time those little eyes open, your child is going to be looking for something familiar to anchor to. As a father, your voice is going to be your identifying feature. So bonding with your baby means talking to your baby. The statistics on how many fathers do not talk or sing to their baby is ridiculously high. Do not be that father. Your newborn wants to hear everything that you have to say and you'll see it when they start to smile, which is around six weeks.

To bond with your baby, you need to use your voice. They don't recognize faces, only that you're a common face. But they do recognize your voice. You were that warm, caring voice that they heard in the womb and next to their mother's voice, yours is so very important to them. So use it. Talk to your baby, hold your baby, and dig down deep and sing to your baby at night to sooth them. It's about being a father to this little child.

For the first three months, you're going to be absorbed with watching your child slowly start to come out of their shell and start exploring their hands and their feet. They don't quite have movement control, but by the end of the first month, you'll see head control. By the end of the third month, they'll definitely be able to look around at stuff. As for hands, let them grab onto your finger, hold their hands, and tickle their little feet. Encourage them to move and show them that they're loved.

Essentially, the first three months are about keeping your baby happy and free from harm.

Past the First Obstacle

The first three months are a lot of trial and error as you begin to understand what it means to be a father and what it means to have a baby. It's a crazy, insane time of your life where you learn how to change diapers, how to give baths, and just how cute a little human can be, even though they sleep most of the time. Now, once you hit that third month, things really start to get interesting, because you've hit your rhythm.

Now, I'm not going to lie to you. This idea that you've figured it out is an illusion that's going to hang around you for years to come. I assure you, that every step of the way, you are in adaptation mode, trying to anticipate what kind of freak transition is on the horizon. But right now, you're relatively safe. You don't have to worry about anything other than truly enjoying this pure, little soul and loving it to the point of absurdity.

At three months, you child is going to be going in for their first new series of shots and it's probably the most painful and horrifying experience of your life. This isn't like the ones they gave in the hospital. Now, I don't care what you read on Facebook or Twitter, vaccinations are vital not only to the survival of your child but to the survival of every other newborn in the world. Do not be the fool who does not vaccinate their child. There is no scientific evidence to support the vaccination conspiracy theories and there's definitely something to worry about if you don't get them vaccinated. Remember, the consequences of not vaccinating your newborn and infant is that they can die. That's not a gamble I was willing to take, nor should you. Be a responsible parent.

Other than that, three to six months is amazing. There are so many things that you're going to experience. You child is going to start cooing and making noises more intentionally. They're going to start trying to sit up. They're going to recognize objects and will start to 'dance' to music that they recognize. Your little bundle of joy is going to start revealing a little personality that is more perfect and beautiful than anything you could have ever imagined.

So let's start off with some basics that you'll need to take care of. By three months, you should definitely have your child transitioning into the crib. This was really hard for me. I loved having my babies next to my bed when I slept, even if they did wake me up in the middle of the night a thousand times. But, at some point we have to let them have their own room. Transitioning them to the crib is tough, but it's actually better for everyone involved. Babies are more likely to sleep longer and more soundly if they can't see or hear mom and dad. So they sleep longer and you get to sleep longer. Score.

Along the lines of sleep, around month three, you should really start setting your baby up to distinguish the difference between night and day. Seriously, this is vitally important for your own sanity and your own health. In the morning, have a ritual to show them that the day has started and that others are awake. At night, develop a ritual that you can perform every night with them to show them that it's time for a long sleep. Sing a song to them, give them a bath, feed them, or do whatever you need to in order to engrain that understanding into their cute little heads. Also, you're going to have to start getting tough.

Around month four and definitely by month five, you need to start letting them cry to sleep. I know this sounds horrible and it truly is for the first few times, but when your baby cries to sleep after the night ritual and you slowly pull back from running to give them a bottle or rock them to sleep, they start to pick up what's going on. They won't hold it against you, they won't become psychopaths, and they definitely won't remember how horrible it was that you made them go to sleep. This honestly sounds cold, heartless, and difficult, but after a week, they understand. Also, it's important that you cut back on the feedings during the night. You don't want them to start expecting food in the middle of the night, because that just makes things harder for you.

So remember, get that sleeping under control.

Next, you're going to start to notice that they're grabbing things and playing with things more. When they're up, they're ready to go and they're more than ready to play with you. So playtime has finally begun. Sing them songs, teach them games like peek-a-boo and the wheels on the bus. Get your child a walker as soon as possible, because they're going to love trying to move around on their own. It's a blast seeing their eyes light up.

By now, your baby is sitting up on their own and it's important to have toys for them so that they can start playing by themselves, or at least experimenting with it. They'll talk to their toys, transition them from hand to hand, and toss them around. This is called self-soothing and self-entertaining. It's vital for them to develop their own sense of independence and not need you holding them for every second of the day. That's another thing, you're going to need to cut down on the holding, just so they know that there are other things to do out there in the big world.

Acquaint them with the outdoors and be sure to take your baby on walks. Babies absolutely love going on adventures and you should relish the times they have. By six months, you'll also be feeding them baby food and getting to watch their reactions to different kinds of flavors. All the while, they'll be talking to you and having a chat.

It's a precious time where things are easy, simple, and you've really hit your routine. Enjoy it while it lasts and make sure that you utilize every second available to you.

Getting Through the First Year

After six months, it's like a completely different human is living in your house. It's almost like someone fired off the starter's pistol and your baby is off developing and starting their new adventures. This is when the easy part of having a baby comes to a close and your little explorer has officially planted their flag on Earth and are ready to get out there. It's amazing, it's crazy, but above all else, it's so much fun.

By now, fatherhood should be something that you're realizing is an ambiguous assignment that's following you until the day you die. Your job is to provide and protect this little cutie that is more than determined to get into trouble, explore new areas, and find out just where your limits are and shove you over them. Patience is vital to being a father and adapting is also crucial. If the first six months have not taught you that and helped you transition from the man you were before to the man that you're going to be now, then you're in for a rude awakening for these coming months. Because you've entered the realm of mobility.

This is where we cue the dramatic music.

By the seventh month of your child's life, you're realizing that they're out growing everything at a horrifying rate, diapers companies are ripping you off, and that Netflix has a horrible selection of children shows that you don't want to kill yourself halfway through. You've probably realized that reading to them every night is an adventure in and of itself when a seven month old wants to turn the pages on Sophie's newest adventure all by herself.

So by the seventh month, you child will be sitting up straight, moving around as best they can while seated, rolling over, and possibly trying to scoot wherever they can. Let me be completely honest with you. The leaning forward and propping themselves up with their hands and the scoot are the harbingers of the end for this peaceful, stationary baby that you once had. It means that they're going to start crawling soon and that means they're going to be everywhere.

Invest in cleaning your carpets and keep them immaculate. Get rid of anything that is possibly a weapon for your infant. Whatever you do, don't leave small things that they can choke on lying around. Mobility is the scariest moment for you as you watch your child moving around and exploring the world without even an ounce of caution or fear. Also, they're just moving so much. You're going to be chasing after them for years to come, so get used to it.

From what I have experienced and what I have heard from others, crawling is a huge lie on television and in movies. When you think of babies, you think of little tykes crawling around. But it hardly lasts. The moment they start crawling is also the moment they start pulling themselves up on furniture and practicing standing. Once the crawling begins, savor it, because soon, they're going to be running and that's when things get interesting. Once they decide to push themselves up, it's just a game of walking.

Walking is incredibly enjoyable and is one of those powerful moments in your life where you feel that wave of pride and disbelief wash over you. It's a strong moment that hits you every time. But it's not the only thing that you have waiting for you to experience during this period.

This is when play really starts to pick up. You're going to be running around and actually playing with your child now. Naps are going to be fewer and communication is going to start to clear up. At this time, you're also going to start hearing them speak words intentionally. Be ready for all sorts of new territory because once that sixth month hits, they go from newborns to tiny little people who have personalities that shine through. It's going to feel like you're discovering some new trait or ability every day that they have.

Thankfully as well, feeding is officially changing to something more substantial and cheaper for you. As far as baby food goes, I'm going to play the safe card and tell you that we made our own baby food or purchased baby food that only had minimal ingredients. Beechnut is a brand that I cannot praise enough. When they say that their flavor is pineapple, pear, and apple, those are the only three ingredients. You want that. Seriously, you don't need special add-ins for your child. Children have been eating fruit and vegetables for centuries without any problems. You'll also want to be cutting back on the bottles of formula or breast milk. This is the time where you're going to start giving them watered down juices instead to help regulate their digestion and hydrate them more effectively.

Finally, let's talk about the value of reading to your child at this point in their development. It's not just something that people have been perpetrating as a myth just to try and get people to read. No, reading is a vital bonding experience that you're robbing from your child if you don't sit down consistently and read with them. It helps them develop mentally, emotionally, and it helps their verbal skills grow. It's something that every parent should encourage in their child and it's something that will definitely help them in the years to come.

But above everything, remember that your child is only this size once and that they are the most perfect and amazing gift you could imagine. Take care of them and savor every little, lasting experience that you have with them.

Past Year One

Once you hit that first birthday, it's something of a miracle that you've lasted this long and you're probably grateful and thankful to the powers that be that your precious little child has survived this long. Congratulations at this point. The first birthday is a great experience, but I feel like it's more of a triumph to parents than it is to the child. You did it. You survived the first year.

If you look back over this past year, you're going to notice that there was a lot of adapting—a lot of figuring it out as you go. One thing that you're also going to realize is that a lot of what people told you didn't really apply to your situation or that your baby was an entirely different situation. That's pretty much what sums up the truth of being a father. It's all about doing whatever you can to make things easier for your family and to make sure that your child is happy and healthy. It's a lot of work, but after you've conquered the first year, you're in the same basic situation for the rest of the obstacles and troubles to come. Hopefully by now, the necessity of patience and adaptation has been completely conveyed to you with its full extent of possibilities.

After your child's first year, they're officially mobile, talking, and eating food that doesn't come out of a bottle. This is one of the standards of the year to come. There's nothing coming up that you aren't completely capable of undertaking and overcoming, no matter how frightening they are.

If you haven't gone through it yet, you're probably in for your first accident by now. A first medical emergency, whether stitches or a nasty fever, is incredibly terrifying. On average, a child gets sick around six times a year, so that means that you're in for a lot of dealing with feeling sickly. Be sure to remain calm whenever your child gets ill. Remaining calm and having a great doctor that you trust are crucial for you surviving any kind of medical situation that might pop up. Remember, children fall down, have accidents, and get ill. Don't freak out too much.

Another thing that's also incredibly important for you to remember is that rather than just protecting your child, you're also their guide to the world that they're still exploring. So don't be afraid of showing them the world around them. Remember that play and exploration is all new to them and that's going to be one of the things you're going to have to prioritize over the coming years. Again, I cannot emphasize this enough, there's a profound need for you to be the person who shows them the world. You are their first association with everything new to them. Even if they find something outside and you're off at work, the moment you come home, they want to share it with you.

As your child begins the next year of their life, they become more curious, more adventurous, and more excited about the world around them. They still don't really understand concepts of the adult world, but they do understand emotions. They understand when to be happy, when to be sad, and everything in between. Make sure that you're giving them absolutely everything that they want, because on the horizon is probably the hardest part of being a parent. Savor this next year, because what's coming is going to be much harder for you.

On the horizon is what so many loving parents have called the Terrible Twos and it's known that for a reason. It doesn't always happen when they turn two, but it's a good milestone to keep your eye on. This is the last year that you're going to have your sweet, innocent, little baby before their paradigm begins to shift for the first time. So I cannot stress it enough: enjoy this time with them and be there for them. Show them the world and keep them safe. It's time to have fun at this point. So get out there and get adventurous.

The Toddler

Outside of having a teenager, I do not think there is a more difficult time in a parent's life than having a toddler. It isn't because they're malicious or that they're intentionally making things difficult. It's just the facts of life.

As a baby, we as parents show them that they are essentially tiny gods. We worship their every triumph, we're waiting on them hand and foot, we protect and care for them, and when they call, we answer. They build this image of the world around them that they're the center of everything, because as a parent, that's how we act. We have to act that way or our poor child will be neglected and traumatized. But, that eventually comes to an end and when your child realizes this is around their second year of life.

With a child becoming older, their responsibilities become more and more solidified. There is a time for things and they no longer get to be an exception to the entire world. When it's time to eat, they have to eat. When it's time for a nap, they have to nap. Essentially, we are pulling the wool off of their eyes and revealing to them that everything they know about the world right now is a lie. We are showing them that they are not the center, that they do not get away with everything, and that there are consequences. Yes, consequences. There are punishments waiting for those who misbehave. So, when your child is screaming at you because they don't want to take a nap, try to have some understanding with them. They are essentially suffering from an identity crisis. It's like they're fallen gods.

Full expressive and completely capable of communications, toddlers do not have the understanding, the reasoning, nor the comprehension level of adults. Do not try to reason with them. Seriously, when your child turns into a teenager, go ahead and reread this chapter, it's basically the same thing. The most infuriating or disturbing thing as a parent is seeing a grown woman or man trying to reason with their toddler. They don't understand. They can't be reasoned with. You are shattering their very world and all they need to do is cope.

But, that isn't a license to yell at them or punish them needlessly. Remember, toddlers are having a bit of an identity and placement crisis and they are entitled to bad days just like you or I. If you toddler starts freaking out in the middle of the store because you won't buy them some kind of sour-gummy treat, tell them why they're not getting it and if it blows up in your face, just remove them from the store. Take them outside for a walk or back to the car to get things right. Don't punish them for not understanding or having a bad day. You're their parent, not their warden.

When it comes to tantrums, some last advice to you is to stay strong. It is very easy for parents to get overwhelmed or surrender to the screaming and shouting of their child. This is the most important thing I can tell you as a parent and this is the time for you to start enacting it. It's called: the united front. You and your wife need to be on the same page about everything. Decide what the punishment system will be. Sometimes a screaming child just needs to be isolated for a while. Sometimes they just need a change of environment. Do you know what the rules are? Secondly, once you are both on the same page when it comes to rules, make sure you never fight in front of your child. Never, not even once. I know we all have different argument or fighting styles and that we all learn from our parents differently, but acknowledge this up front and address it. It is vital that you at least put up the veneer of unity when it comes to your child. Do not yell, scream, or shout, in front of your child. Not only is this damaging to them, but it is something they will hone in on and exploit in years to come. Do not sew these seeds. Being a parent is hard enough. Don't make it harder on yourself.

Now, I know that I've pretty much made the toddler time sound like living in a house with a psychopath, and sometimes it does feel that way, but it's actually a lot of fun too. They begin to learn new words and try them out. They mispronounce things and they try to understand new concepts. Genuine interests begin to form and you have the opportunity to cultivate and nurture those interests, fanning them into flame. These hobbies or interests could seriously last them a lifetime, so don't shun them. Make your child feel safe and free to expose you to what they're interested in. These traits that children begin to exhibit in the toddler years are seeds that grow and flower over the coming years.

The toddler years are not so bad when you look back on them. Yes, there are days that test the limits of what you call sanity and yes, you're probably going to get food thrown across you, but think of it this way: diapers should be gone by now! Yes, by the time your child is two, you need to have completed or at least started potty training. We started just the month before their second birthday with my children and it worked like a charm. There are lots of great products and methods for you to start using to help your child transition and once you're done with diapers, you can't help but smile. Yes, that is a huge silver lining. Trust me, you'll understand when you start dropping fifty bucks a month on poop bags.

It's important for you to enjoy every possible moment you can with your child and at this point, it's time to also start teaching them about the world. More importantly, it's a very good time to discuss manners and how to act around people. Your child is smart and they are more than capable of saying thank you and you're welcome to people they interact with. Be sure to teach them to be open and how to make friends with other kids at the park, play ground, or at whatever church or communal events you attend. Just remember, you're the gateway to the world and they're going to be watching and learning from you all the time.

Beyond!

Once you've made it past two, you're in pretty smooth sailing. Your child is learning, you're adapting to all the new fads, TV shows, and other oddities that come your way. Essentially, you're going to have a blast until you approach thirteen. That's when most children start to exhibit the teenage attitude, but there's going to have to be an entirely new book on that topic right there. The bottom line is: the hardest part about becoming a father is actually growing to understand the responsibilities and everything that comes with this new, profound territory. It's a big, scary world, but it's yours now.

Being a father is about adaptation and about making the most of the opportunities that are given to you. It's a scary world and there are a lot of challenges that you're going to face along the way, but they are very easy to overcome if you simply put your mind to it and you anticipate the needs that are coming. The thing that I think all fathers need to know is that it is a rare and wonderful privilege to be a father and it should never be taken lightly.

I have known terrible and stupid men who honestly baffled me as to how they survived day to day transition into amazing and respectable fathers. There's something about the responsibility that changes men and brings the best out in them. I would challenge you to find what is great about you and harness that into your fathering skills. Don't be afraid to be creative and step outside the box of what you're used to doing. Nothing will ever be the same once you hold that innocent, lost little child in your hands for the first time. So be ready for the great and wonderful changes that are on your way.

Remember as well that being a father is about learning and changing the way you think about things. Constantly find new material to stimulate you and challenge you. The better you're prepared, the better chance you'll have at staying on top of everything that is coming your way. You don't want any surprises on the horizon and if you find one, you want to have some idea how to handle it before it overwhelms you.

Finally, the one thing that I want to encourage you to do is to remind yourself every day to make the most of your child. There are thousands of people who will never know the love and the wonder that is being a parent and they will never have the chance that you have. Make the most of the precious gift that you've been given and make sure that your child's life is the best, most wonderful, and the most exciting that it can be for them. They look to you for everything and you should make sure that every day is spent giving them exactly what they deserve. They are walking miracles, so don't forget to treat them as such.

Above all, love them profoundly.

Thank you again for buying this book!

I hope this book was able to help you to get an idea about what to expect with fatherhood.

The next step is to start getting into gear.

Finally, if you enjoyed this book, then I'd like to ask you for a favor, would you be kind enough to leave a review for this book on Amazon? It'd be greatly appreciated!

Thank you and good luck!

Made in the USA
Lexington, KY
13 December 2016